Rig it Right Essentials

Bass

CHAD FOSTER

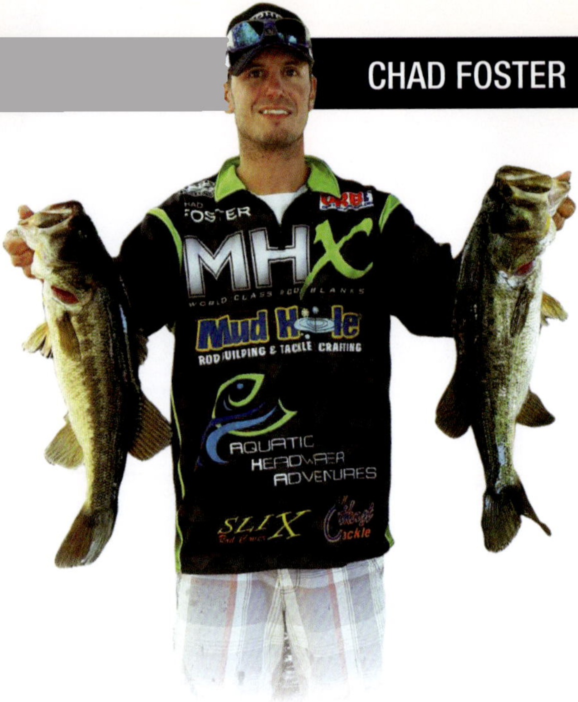

Aquatic Headwater Adventures Fishing Guide
Kissimmee, Florida.

USCG Master Captain
Avid Tournament Angler
Youth Fishing Lessons Teacher
Local Circuit Angler of the Year Titles

INTRODUCTION

There are a number of Black Bass species in North America, including smallmouth, spotted, redeye, Suwannee, shoal and Guadalupe, but perhaps the best known and most revered is Micropterus salmoides, or Largemouth Bass.

The largemouth (along with spotted and smallmouth to a lesser extent) is responsible for the growth of a multibillion dollar industry that has seen the development of specialised fishing equipment beyond any other species in the USA.

The largemouth is the largest and most abundant of all black bass in North America. From your small neighborhood ponds and stream to the complex reservoirs, rivers, and lakes across the country, angling opportunities will exist. The northern US states are where you can catch huge numbers, (I mean 100 to 150 fish a day). But it's the warmer southern states from California to Florida and everything in between where you'll find a bass of a lifetime.

Bass are a fierce and spectacular fighting fish and opportunistic feeders preying on frogs, crawfish, minnows, other fish, and virtually any creature that is small enough for them to swallow on or below the water's surface.

This booklet will show you the best rigs to use, how to rig them, plus where, how and when to fish them.

Good fishing, Chad.

CONTENTS

ALABAMA RIG

WHEN TO FISH

Fish anytime bass are suspended in the water column or schooled up.

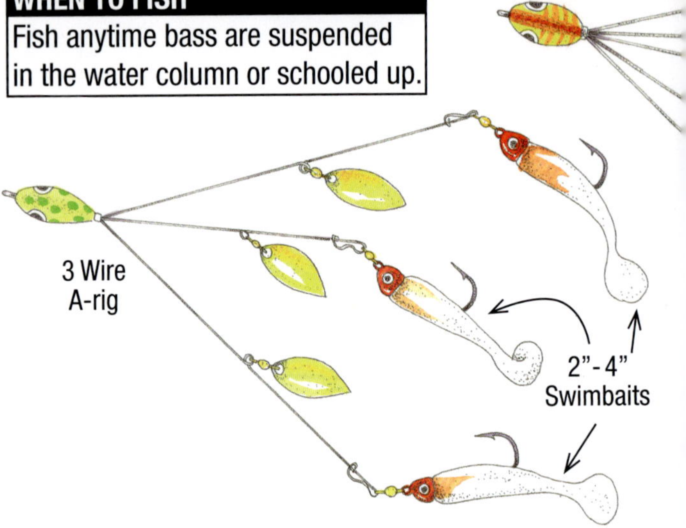

A killer rig for catching suspended fish. Slowly retrieve through water column.

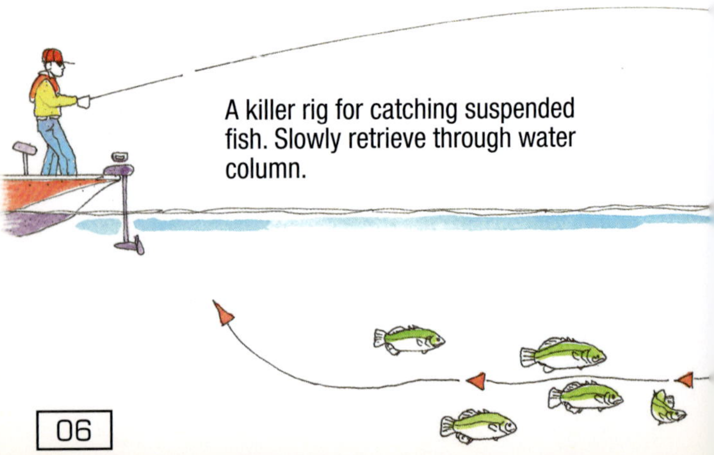

Count the rig down to the desired depth before retrieving.

TIP

Match the swimbait trailers to the baitfish that the bass are feeding on. Always try and 'match the hatch'.

BUZZBAIT

WHEN TO FISH

Topwater buzzers work best in spring and fall when water temperatures are between 55 and 70 degrees Fahrenheit.

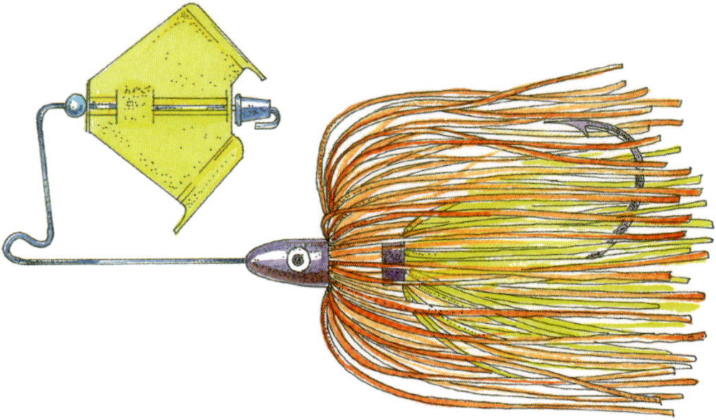

Topwater lures can be used anywhere. Schooling bass often fall victim to topwater baits.

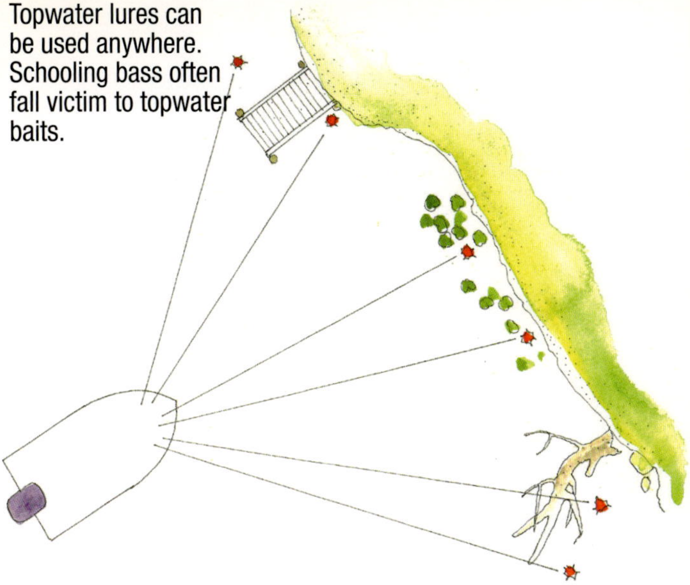

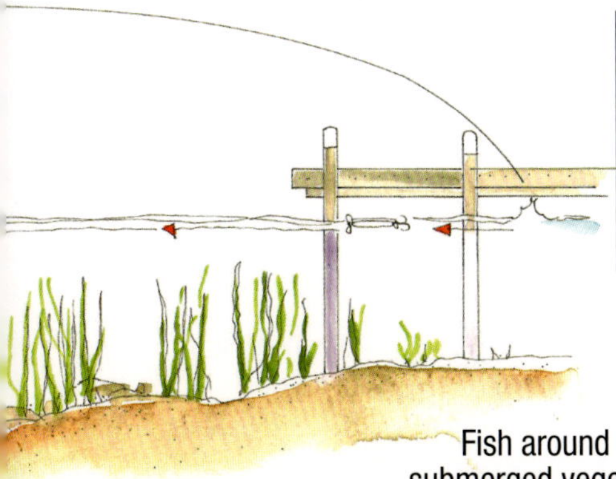

TIP

Don't rule out using buzzbaits in the dog days of summer.

Fish around docks, submerged vegetation, wood and any other cover.

CAROLINA RIG

WHEN TO FISH

The Carolina Rig is productive all year round. Fish when bass are holding close to the bottom.

TIP

Drag slowly along the bottom. It is especially productive when there is current.

Slowly drag Carolina Rig over small rocks, shell beds and through scattered grass. This type of structure and cover located on a baron flat can be a hotspot for bass.

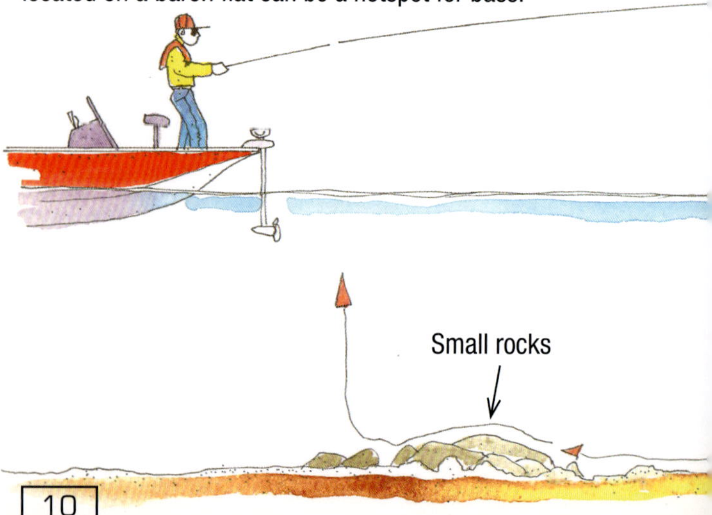

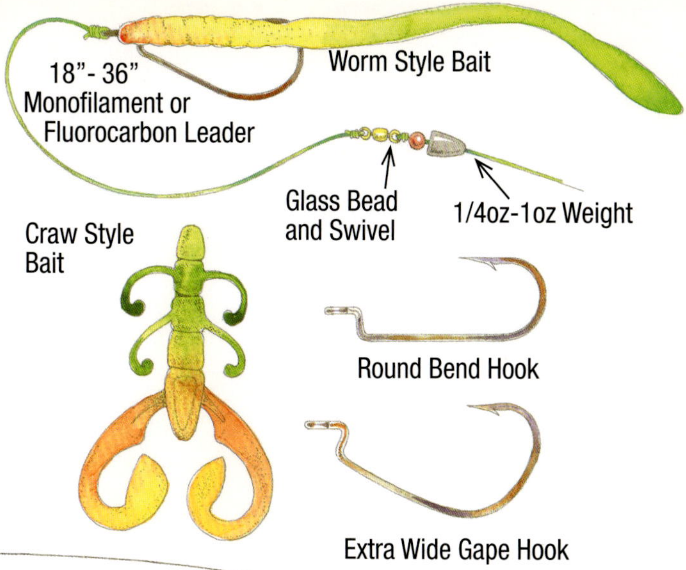
Worm Style Bait
18"- 36"
Monofilament or
Fluorocarbon Leader
Glass Bead
and Swivel
1/4oz-1oz Weight
Craw Style
Bait
Round Bend Hook
Extra Wide Gape Hook

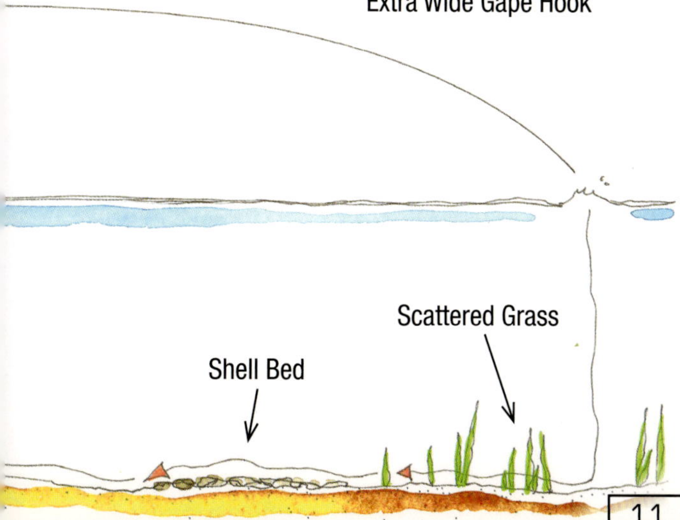
Scattered Grass
Shell Bed

BLADED JIG
(CHATTERBAIT)

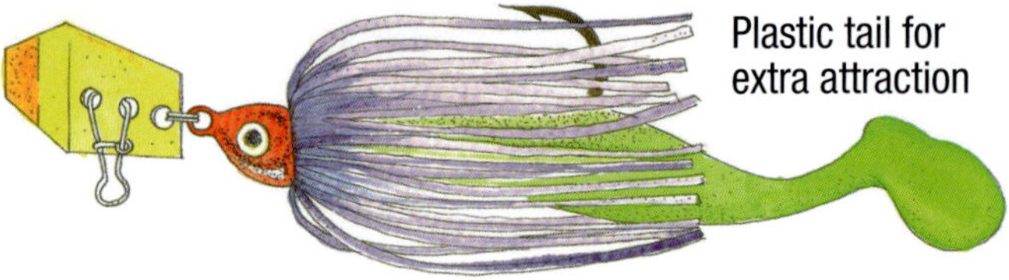

Plastic tail for extra attraction

1/4 - 3/4oz sizes

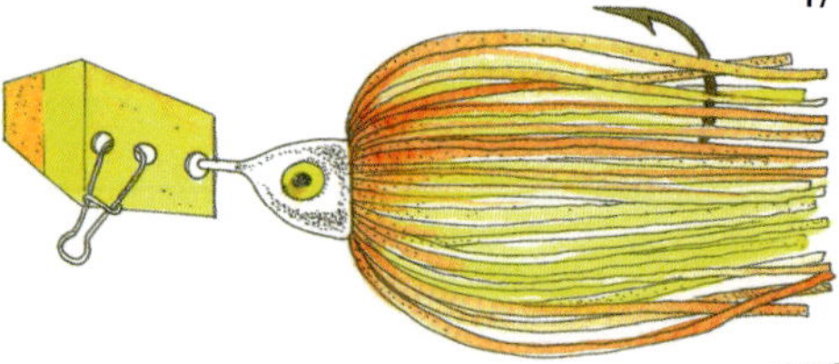

Steady retrieves will produce but often a reel, twitch, pause retrieve will increase results. Ripping the bait free from grass will produce reaction strikes.

WHEN TO FISH

Bladed Jigs are a good choice anytime but excel in spring and fall.

Cast parallel to weed edge keeping lure in strikezone maximizing opportunity to get bitten.

TIP

Don't rule out the inside of the weed flat

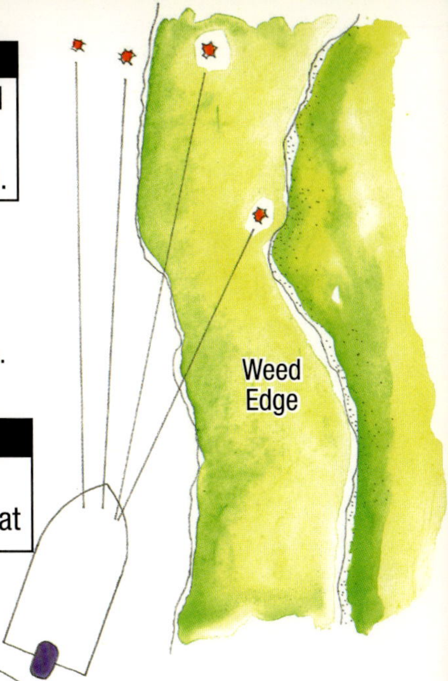

TIP

Keep the jig in contact with the grass to maintain the Bladed Jigs full potential.

CRANKBAITS

WHEN TO FISH

Crankbaits excel everyday of the year on bass in any water color and at any depth.

Deep Diver

Square Bill

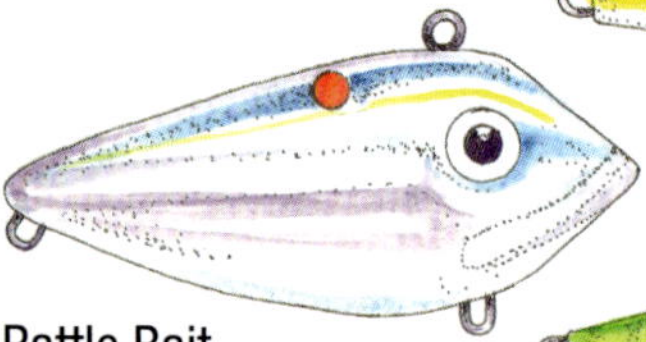

Rattle Bait
(Best when ripped through grass)

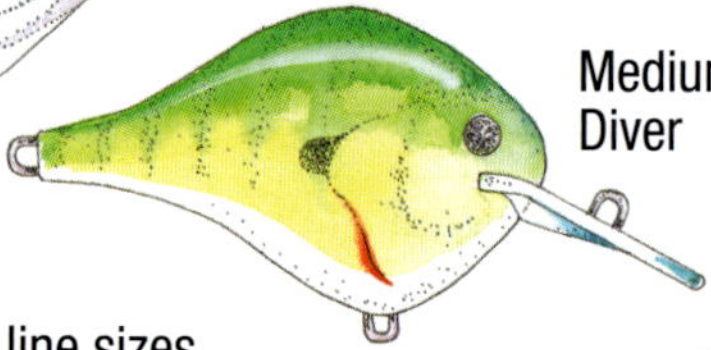

Medium Diver

Experiment with different line sizes to obtain more or less depth from your crankbait.

Experiment with different casting angles.

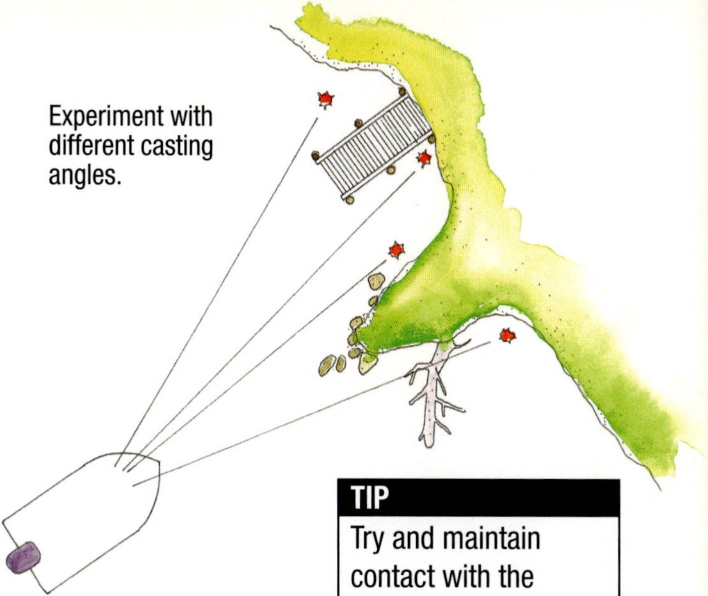

TIP

Try and maintain contact with the bottom, structure or any submerged grass for added success.

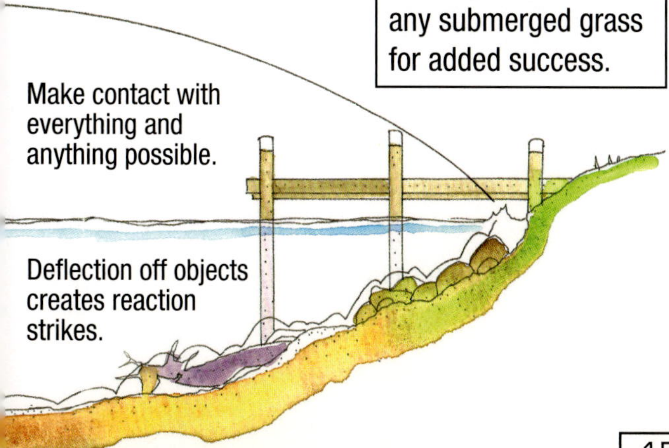

Make contact with everything and anything possible.

Deflection off objects creates reaction strikes.

DROP SHOT

WHEN TO FISH

Every day of the year, rain or shine, there is never a wrong time to fish a Drop Shot rig.

TIP

Try 'Wacky' rigging your Drop Shot bait for a different look. Use light fishing line to optimise results.

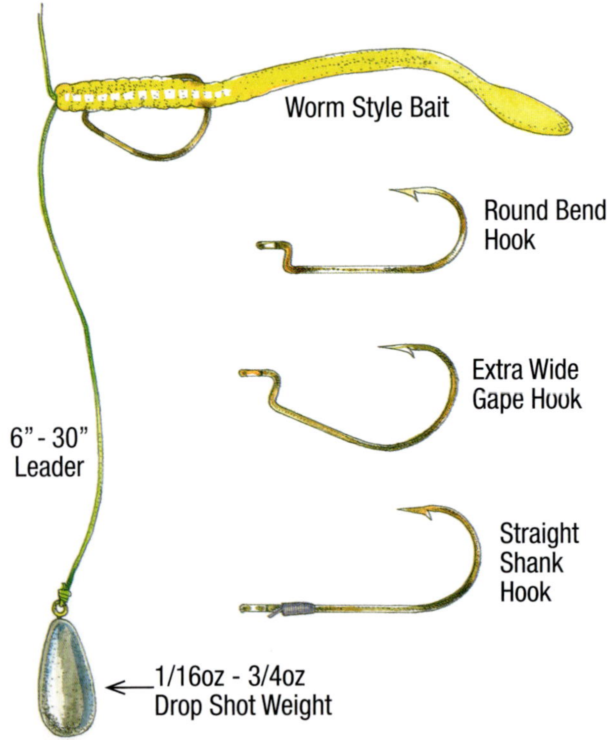

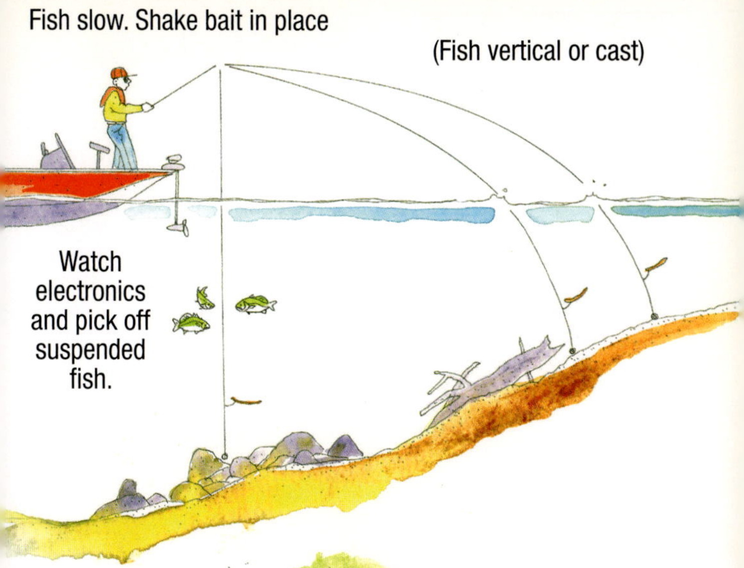
Fish slow. Shake bait in place
(Fish vertical or cast)
Watch electronics and pick off suspended fish.

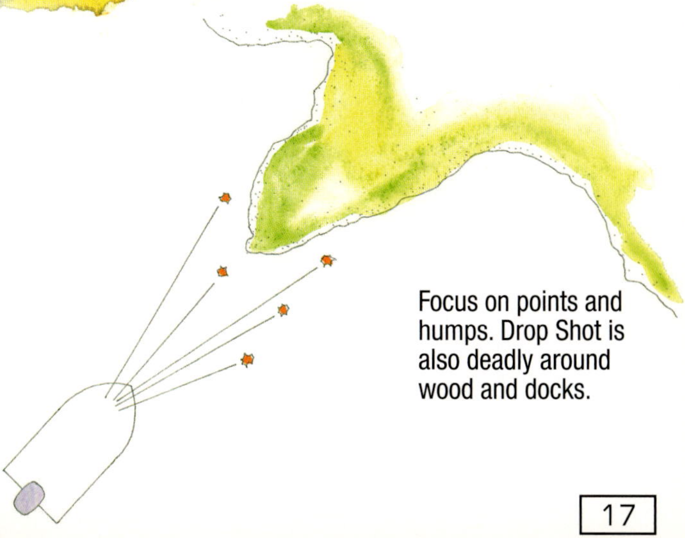
Focus on points and humps. Drop Shot is also deadly around wood and docks.

FLOAT A FLY

WHEN TO FISH

The Float A Fly rig is a deadly technique during the winter months and in clear water.

Float A Fly is a wintertime technique for when the fish are lethargic due to cold water temperatures.

Fish slow with an occasional jig of the rod tip to add slight action to the fly.

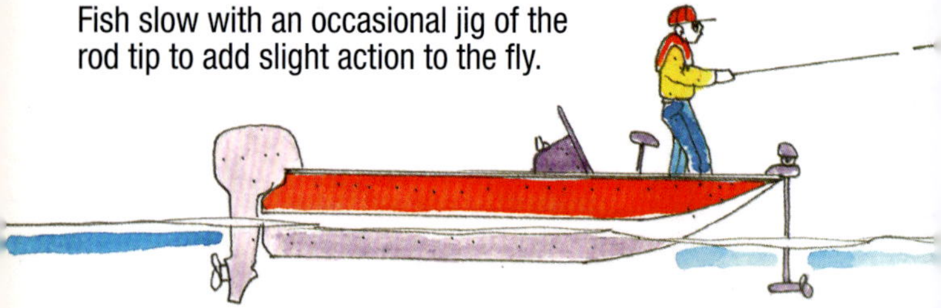

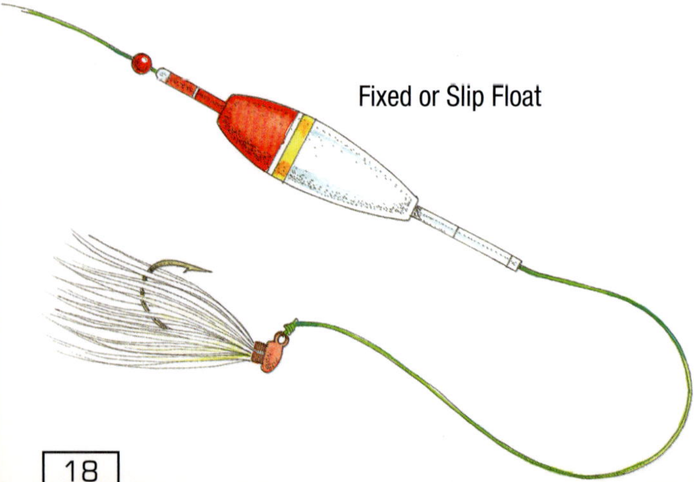

TIP

Fish near the sharpest breaks available. Adjust the float to hover the hair jig just above where the bass are holding in the water column.

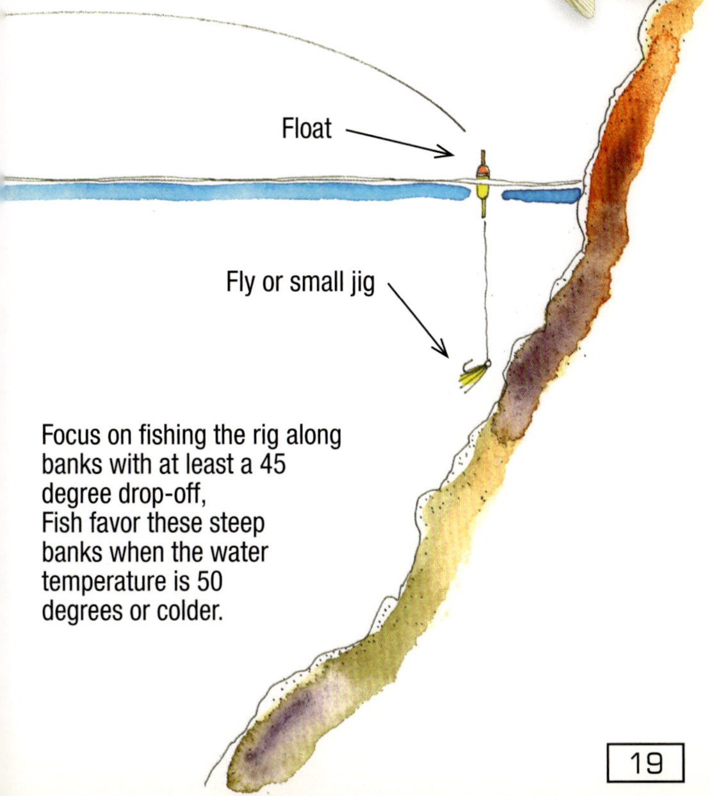

Focus on fishing the rig along banks with at least a 45 degree drop-off, Fish favor these steep banks when the water temperature is 50 degrees or colder.

FROGGIN

WHEN TO FISH

Frogs are a great choice around emergent vegetation in spring, summer and fall. The optimum water temperature is anything over 55 degrees Fahrenheit.

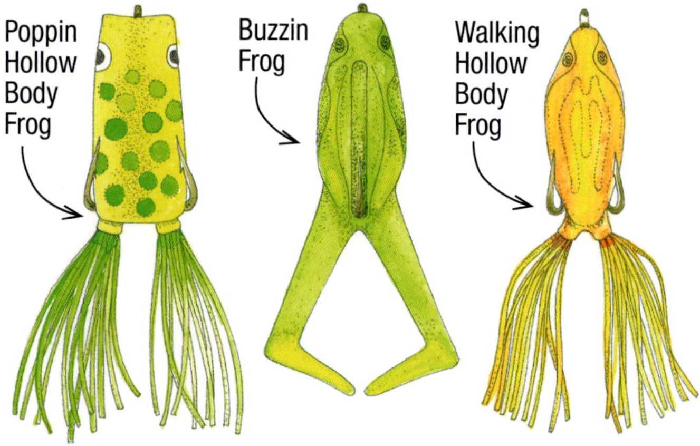

Don't hesitate to cast under docks and flooded brush.

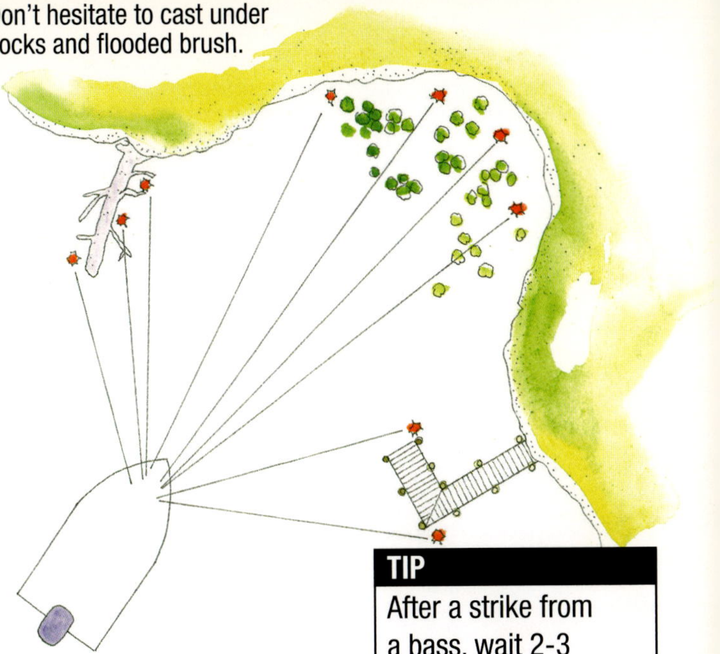

TIP

After a strike from a bass, wait 2-3 seconds before setting the hook to increase your hookup percentage.

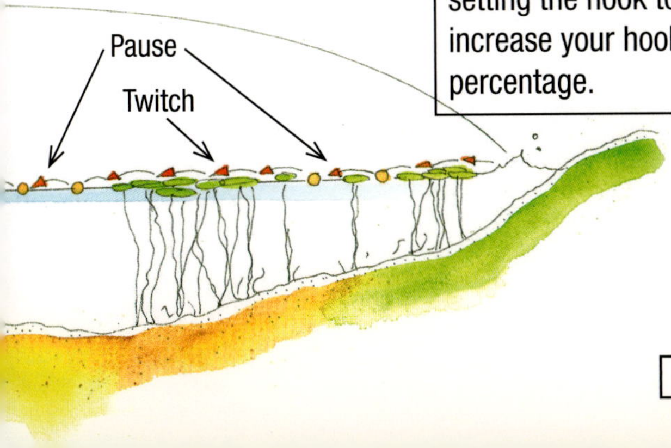

GRUBBIN

WHEN TO FISH

Grubbin excels during winter, fall and spring. Smallmouth bass love this technique.

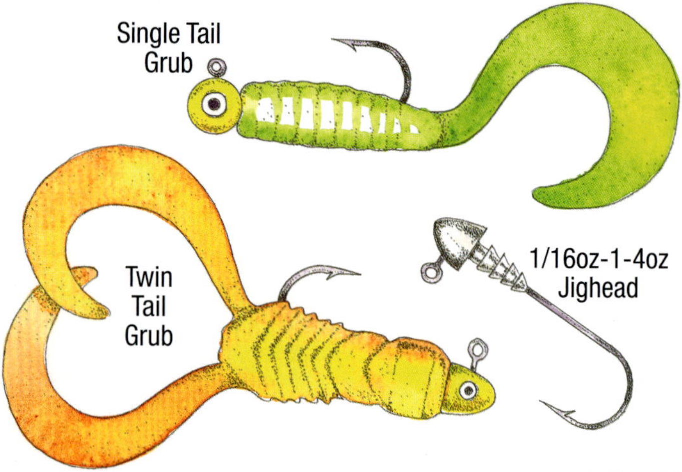

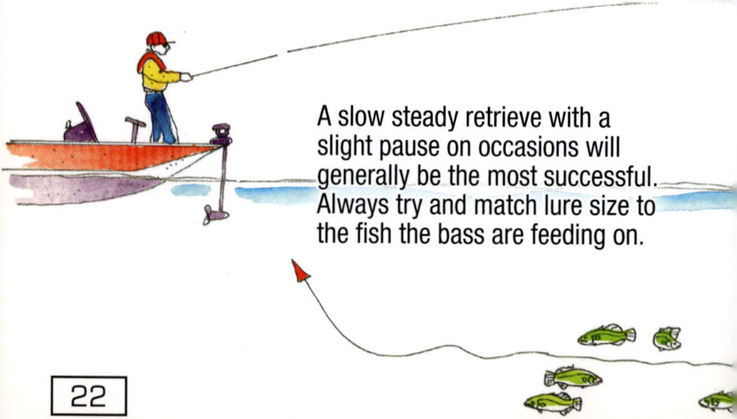

A slow steady retrieve with a slight pause on occasions will generally be the most successful. Always try and match lure size to the fish the bass are feeding on.

Grubs and Swimbaits work great when probing around shallow cover in search of big bass.

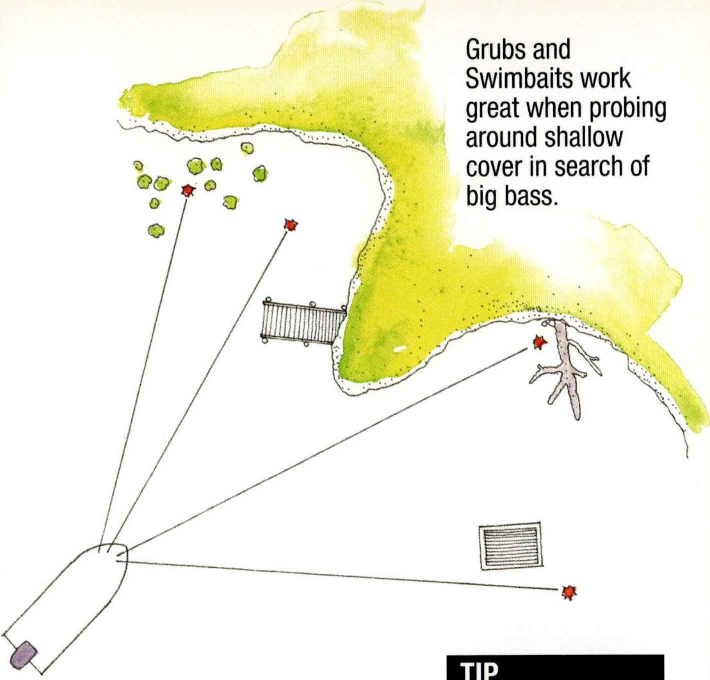

TIP

Great for fish suspended in the water column.

Count down to the depth at which fish have been located on your electronics.

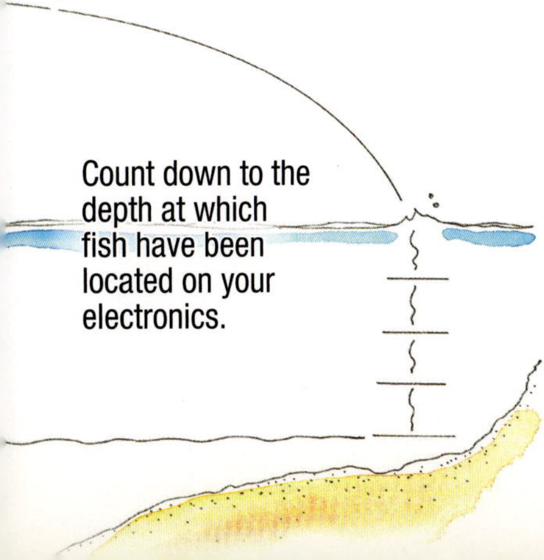

JERKBAIT

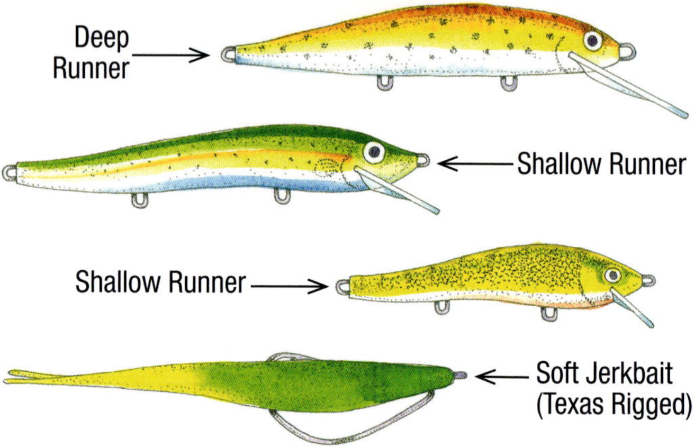

Deep Runner
Shallow Runner
Shallow Runner
Soft Jerkbait (Texas Rigged)

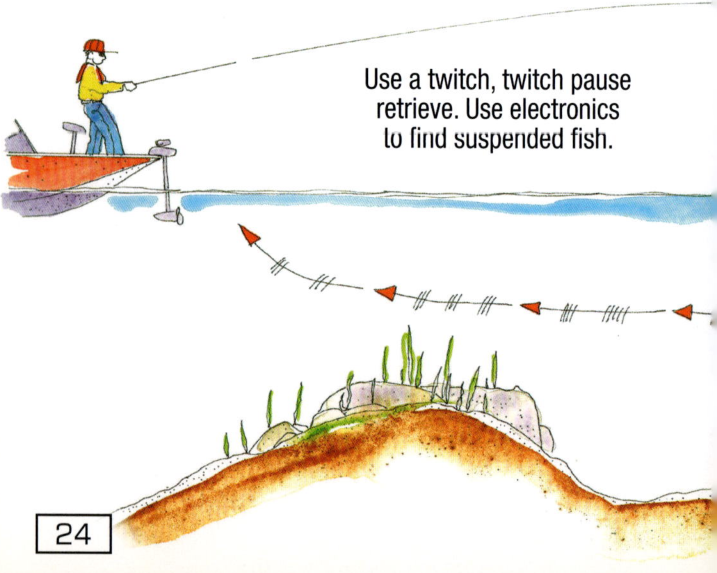

Use a twitch, twitch pause retrieve. Use electronics to find suspended fish.

WHEN TO FISH

Jerkbaits are an amazing all season bait. Suspended bass chasing bait have a difficult time resisting these erratic lures.

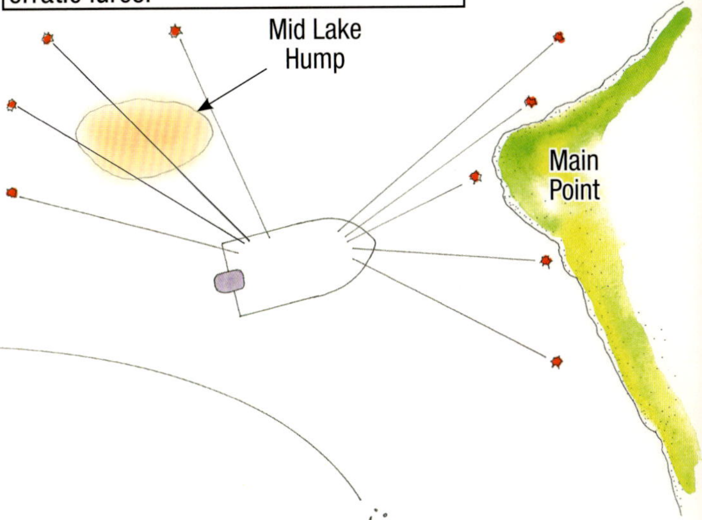

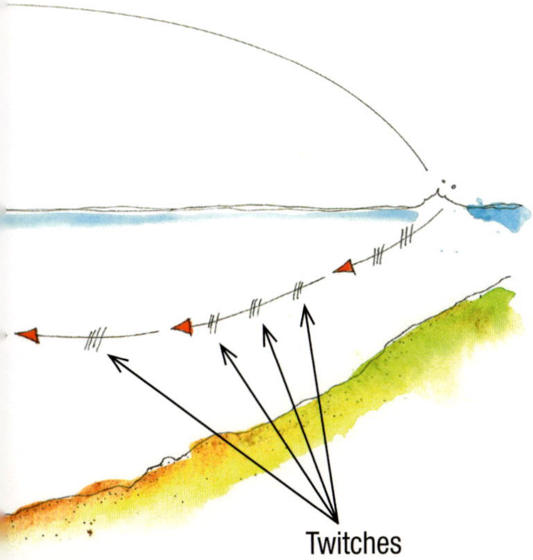

TIP

Vary your retrieve speed. Generally slow in cold water and fast in warm water.

PUNCHING
(PLUNKIN)

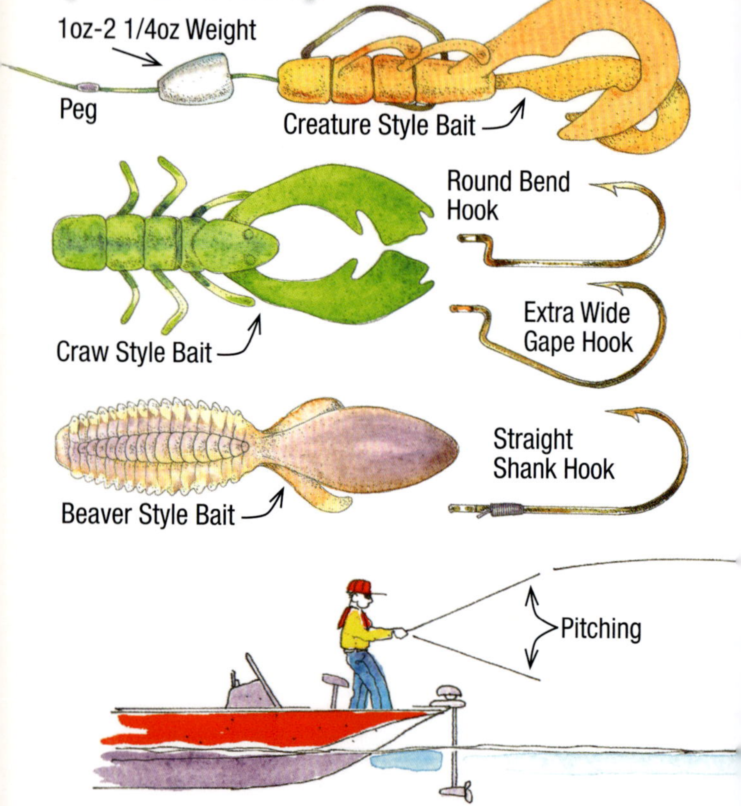

Punch through mat with heavy weight. Work bait up and down.

WHEN TO FISH

Don't be afraid to fish this rig all year round. Punching excels in matted-up vegetation.

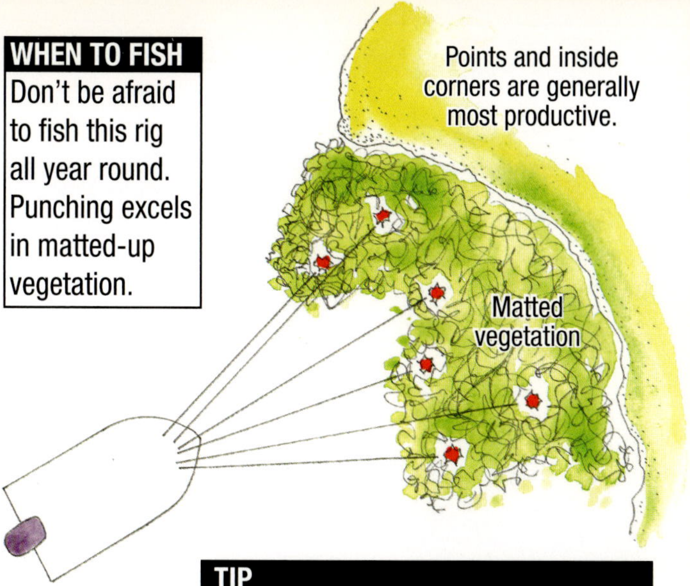

TIP

Use the lightest weight possible, but still allowing you to punch through the thickest looking part of the mat.

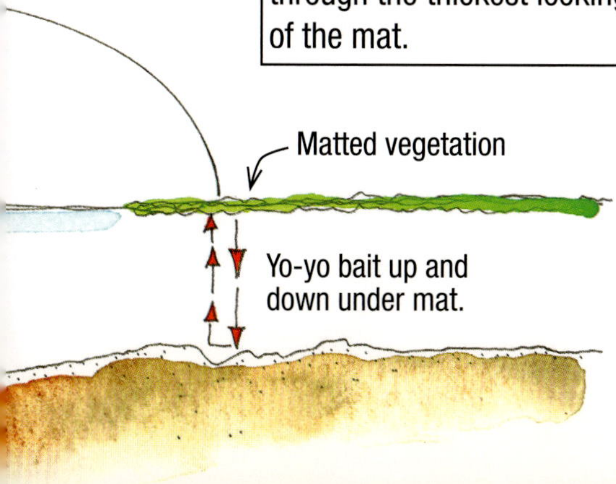

SCROUNGER HEAD

WHEN TO FISH

Scrounger heads work best in spring, summer and fall. Throw a Scrounger in the same locations as a Spinnerbait and Chatterbait when offering fish an alternative.

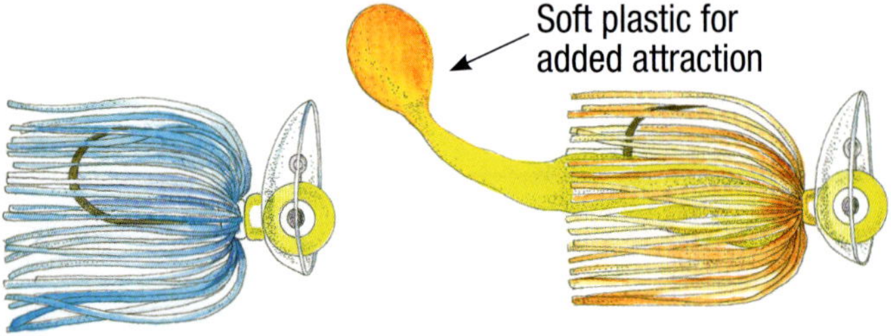

Steady retrieve will produce but often a reel, twitch, pause retrieve will increase results. Ripping the bait free from grass will produce reaction strikes.

TIP

Tip a Scrounger with a soft plastic of your choice for added action and increased success.

Cast parallel to weed edge keeping lure in strikezone maximizing opportunity to get a bite.

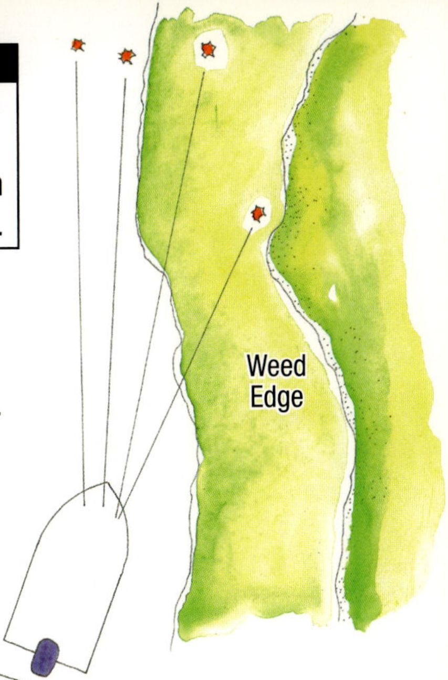

SHAKY HEAD

WHEN TO FISH

24/7 everyday of the year! The Shaky Head will catch fish in any cover anywhere. Big and little fish will just eat it.

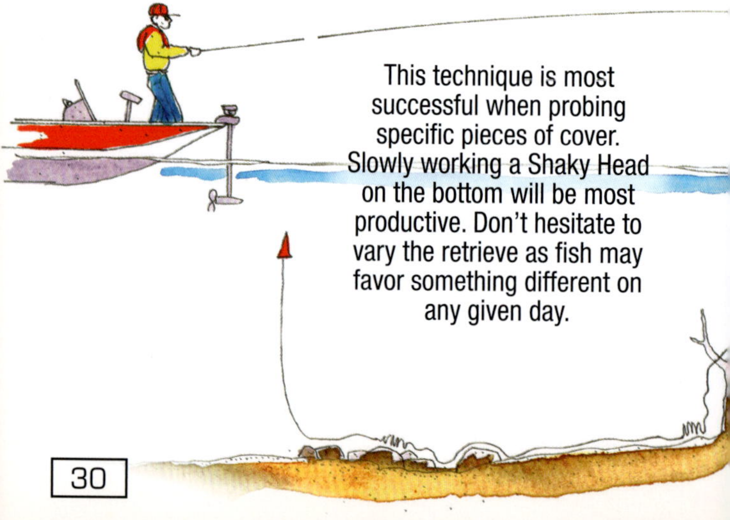

This technique is most successful when probing specific pieces of cover. Slowly working a Shaky Head on the bottom will be most productive. Don't hesitate to vary the retrieve as fish may favor something different on any given day.

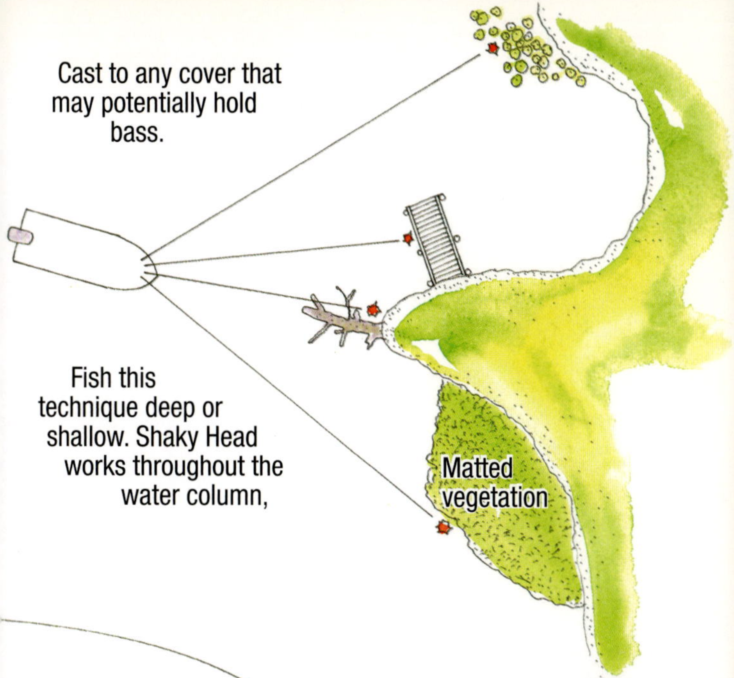

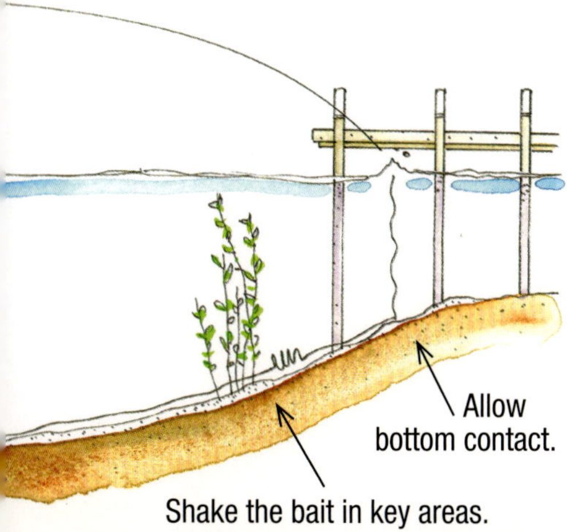

TIP

Fish slow using 6-10 pound line & a spinning outfit for best results.

SKIRTED JIGS

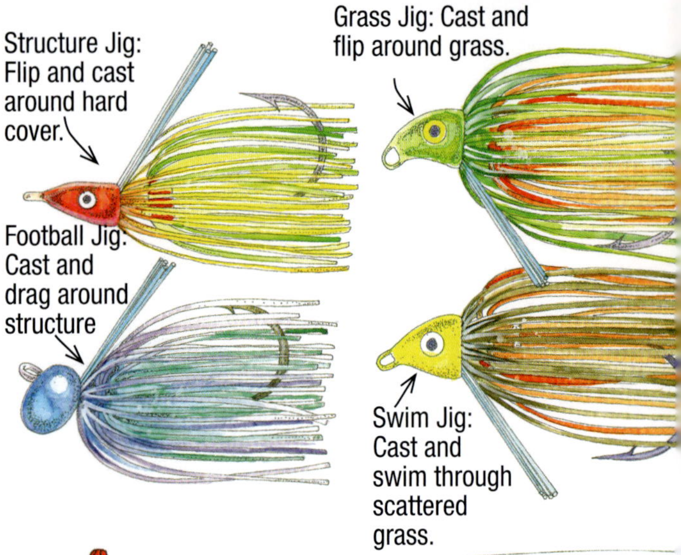

Rubber skirted jigs can be hopped, drug, swam, dead sticked, or stroked. There is no wrong way to fish a jig. Always remember to experiment with your retrieve.

Cast to any cover that may potentially hold bass.

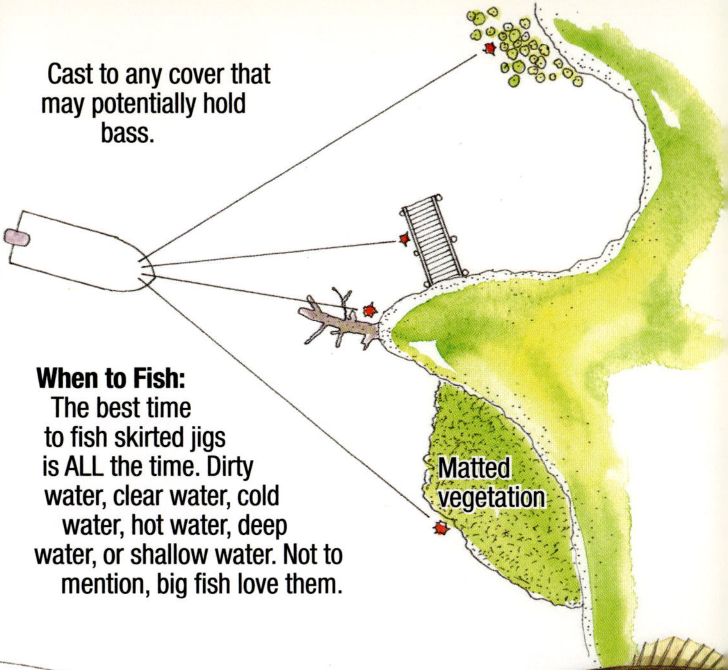

When to Fish:
The best time to fish skirted jigs is ALL the time. Dirty water, clear water, cold water, hot water, deep water, or shallow water. Not to mention, big fish love them.

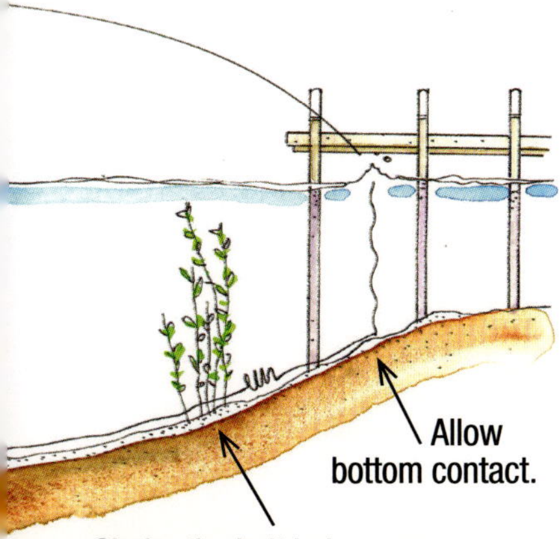

TIP

In dark stained or muddy water, focus on darker colors. In clear water, focus on lighter natural colors.

SPINNER BAIT

WHEN TO FISH

Spinner baits work best when the water temperature is over 55 degrees Fahrenheit. Pre-spawn and fall is when it shines.

TIP

Use an erratic retrieve. Willow Blades work best in clear water and Colorado Blades work best in dirty water.

Always try keeping contact with available cover. Spinner Baits are not only great baits around grass, they come through and around wood with ease.

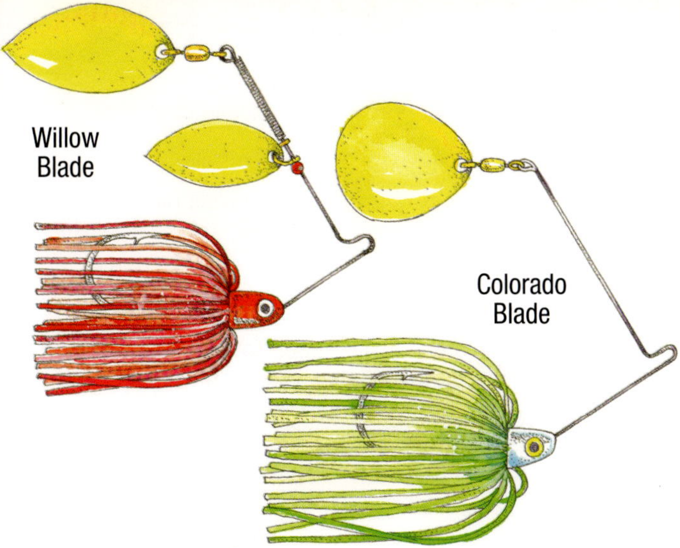
Willow
Blade
Colorado
Blade

SPLIT SHOT RIG

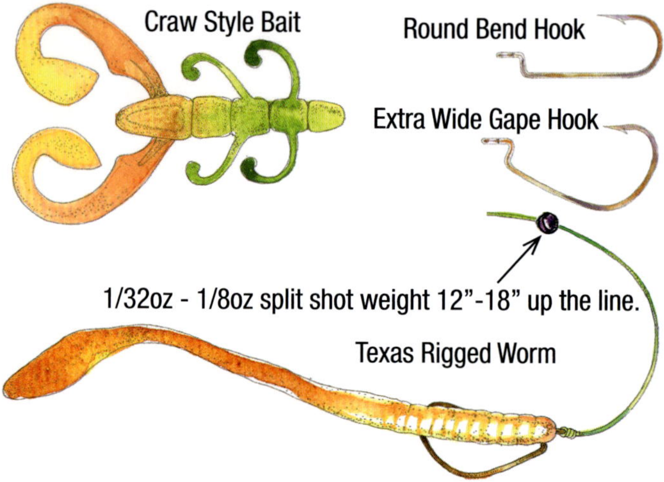

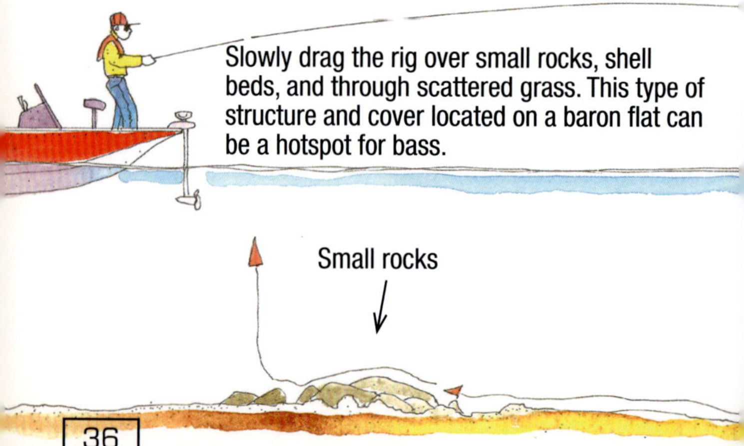

Slowly drag the rig over small rocks, shell beds, and through scattered grass. This type of structure and cover located on a baron flat can be a hotspot for bass.

WHEN TO FISH

Anytime you're faced with areas containing shallow scattered submerged grass is when this rig excels. This finesse rig also works great on heavily pressured bass.

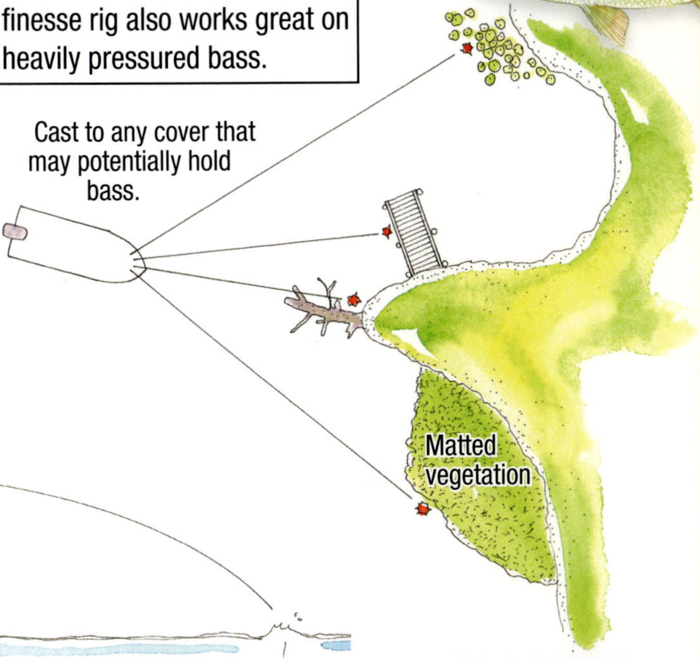

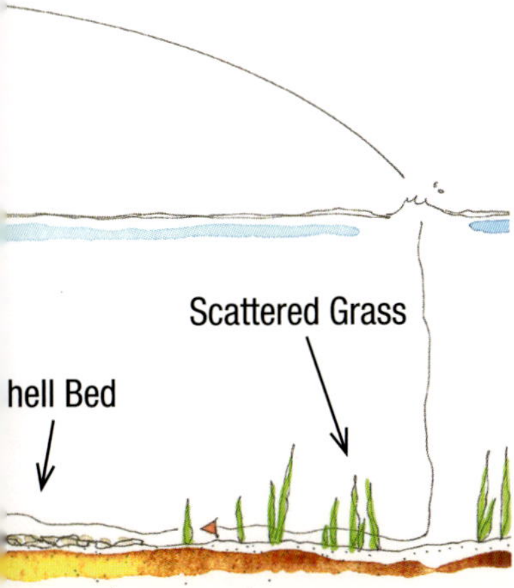

TIP

Fish with light line and drag slowly along the bottom. The bites tend to be very light so concentrate.

SPOON

WHEN TO FISH

Bass love spoons, in all seasons from winter through to summer. These pieces of metal work great on fish suspended out in open water.

Spoons are very productive when jigged vertically through suspended bass.

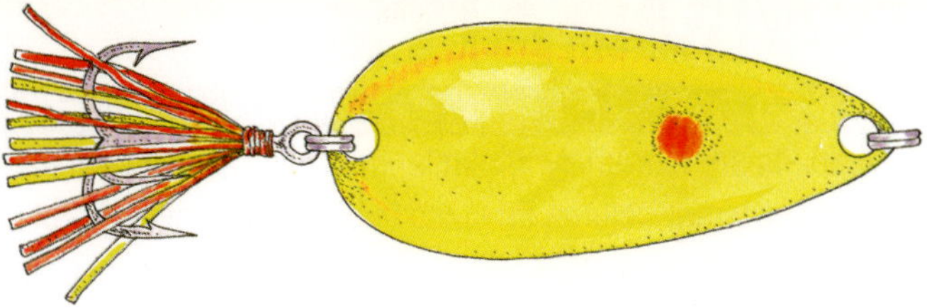

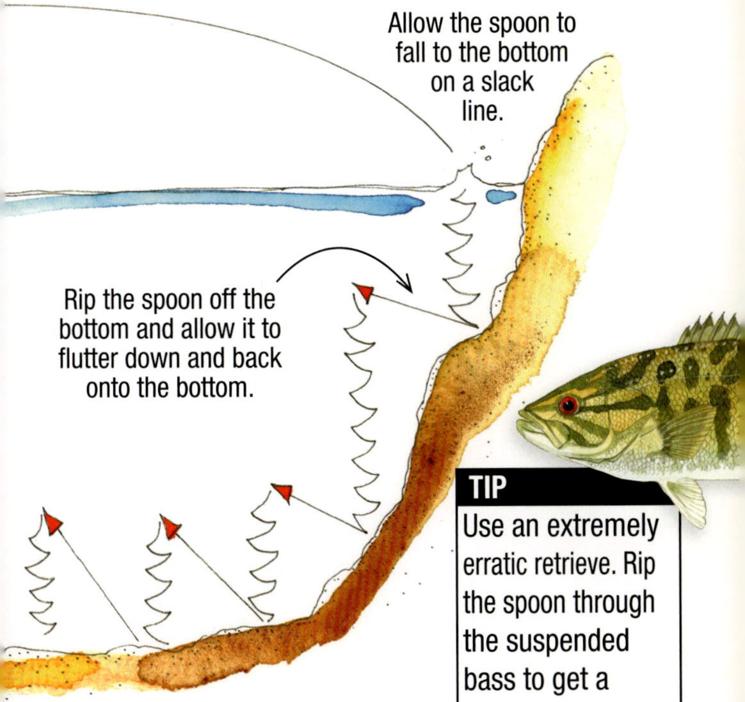

TIP

Use an extremely erratic retrieve. Rip the spoon through the suspended bass to get a 'reaction' bite.

SWIMBAITS

WHEN TO FISH

Swimbaits are extremely versatile; they can be fished in any part of the water column and also in all water temperatures. They can be fished in open water and around the thickest cover.

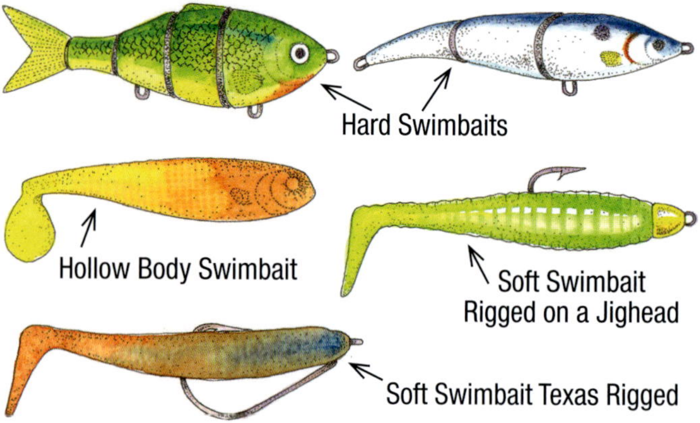

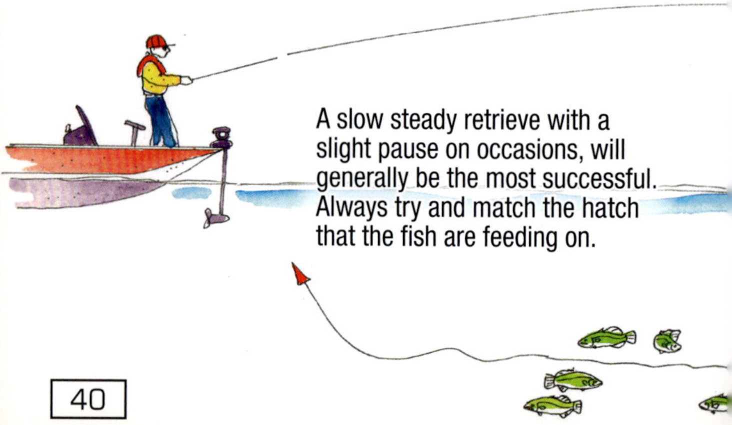

A slow steady retrieve with a slight pause on occasions, will generally be the most successful. Always try and match the hatch that the fish are feeding on.

Swimbaits work great when probing around shallow cover in search of big bass.

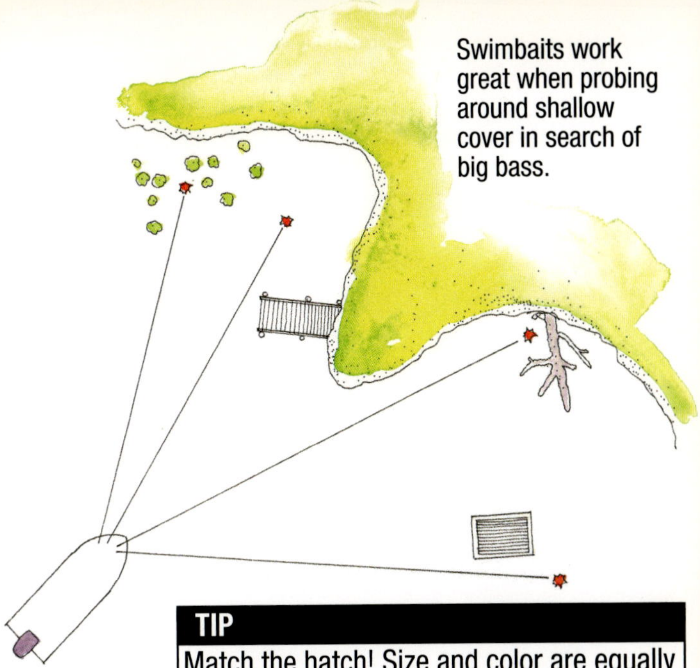

TIP

Match the hatch! Size and color are equally important when matching the hatch.

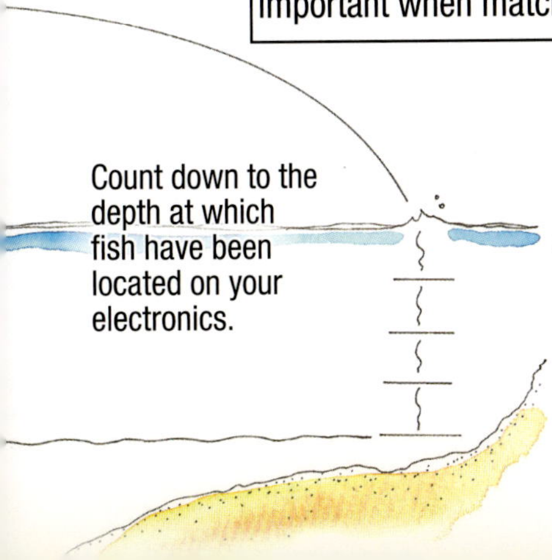

Count down to the depth at which fish have been located on your electronics.

TEXAS RIG

WHEN TO FISH

A texas rig is the most versatile rig in bass fishing. Fish this technique in every situation possible and you will see results.

This technique is most successful when probing specific pieces of cover. Slowly working a Texas Rig on the bottom tends to be the most productive technique. Don't hesitate to vary your retrieve

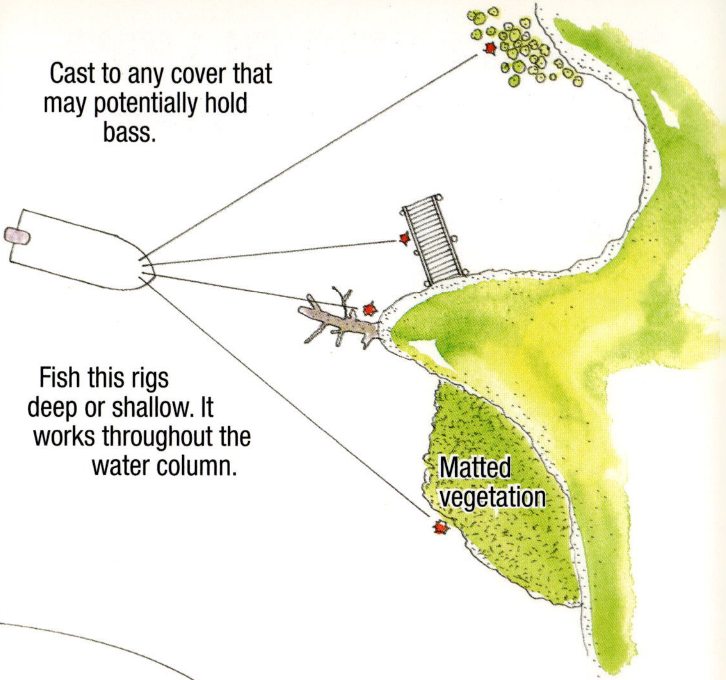

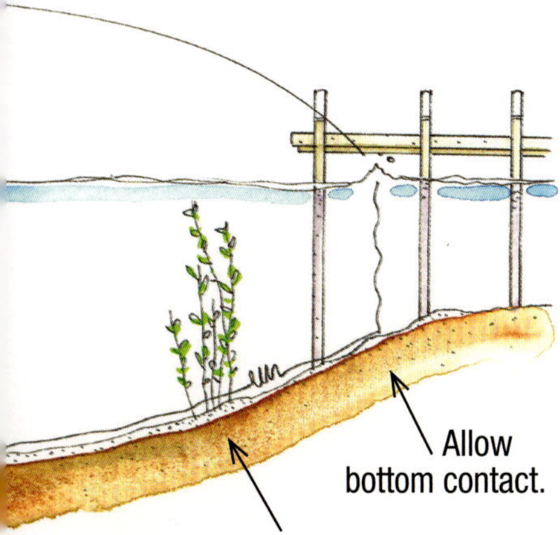

TIP

With the ability to hide the hook point making this rig virtually snag free, don't be afraid to cast a Texas Rig anywhere.

TOPWATER PLUGS

WHEN TO FISH

Topwater Plugs are productive baits in a wide variety of conditions, although they really shine around the spawn and fall of the year.

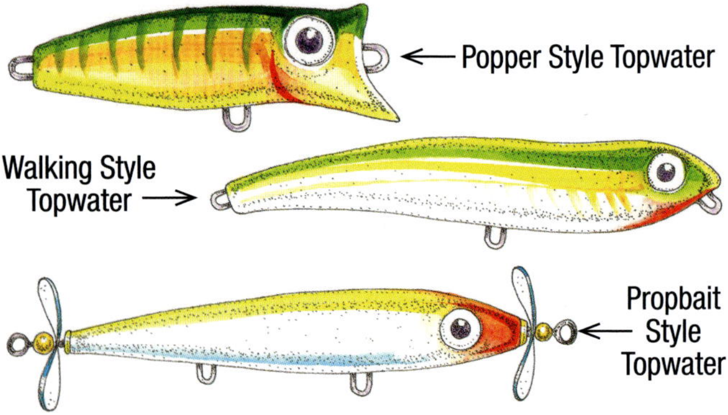

Topwater lures can be used anywhere. Suspended schooling fish are great targets for topwater baits.

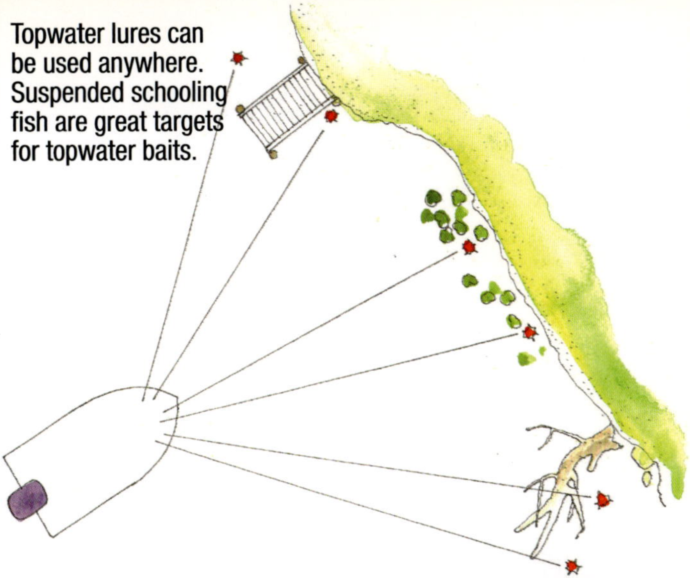

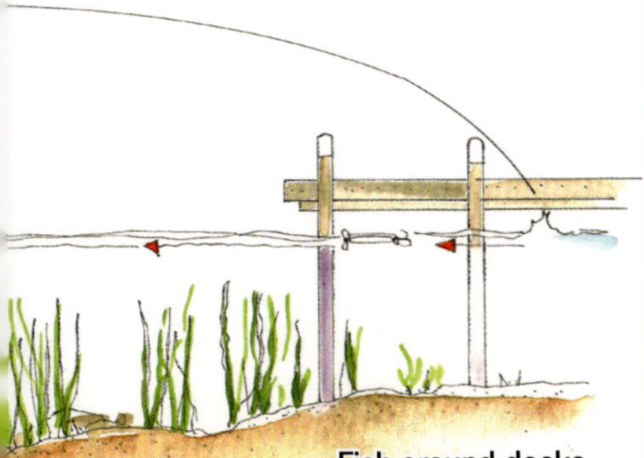

Fish around docks, submerged vegetation, wood and any other cover.

TIP

Try a Topwater Plug on those slick, calm, sunny days when nothing else seems to be productive; you might just be surprised with the result.

WACKY RIG

WHEN TO FISH

Wacky Rig is great in all fishing conditions, but it excels during the spawn season.

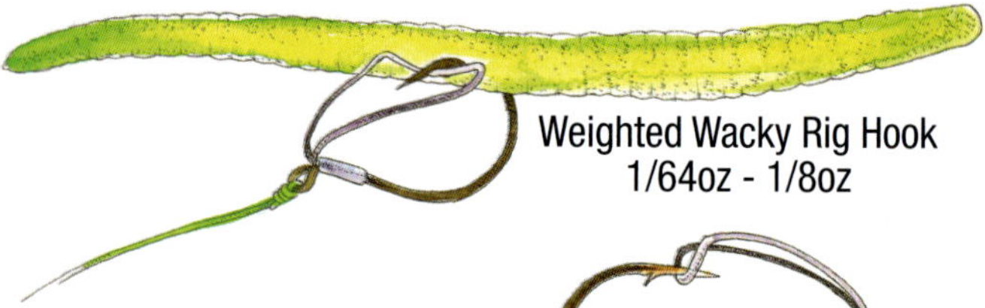

Weighted Wacky Rig Hook
1/64oz - 1/8oz

Weedless Wacky
Rig Hook

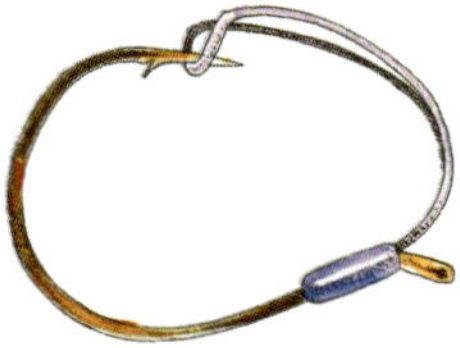

Cast the out the Wacky Rig and allow the bait the hit the bottom (you will get 80% of your hits on the fall) If the strike does not occur on the first fall, then retrieve the rig to the surface and allow to fall again.

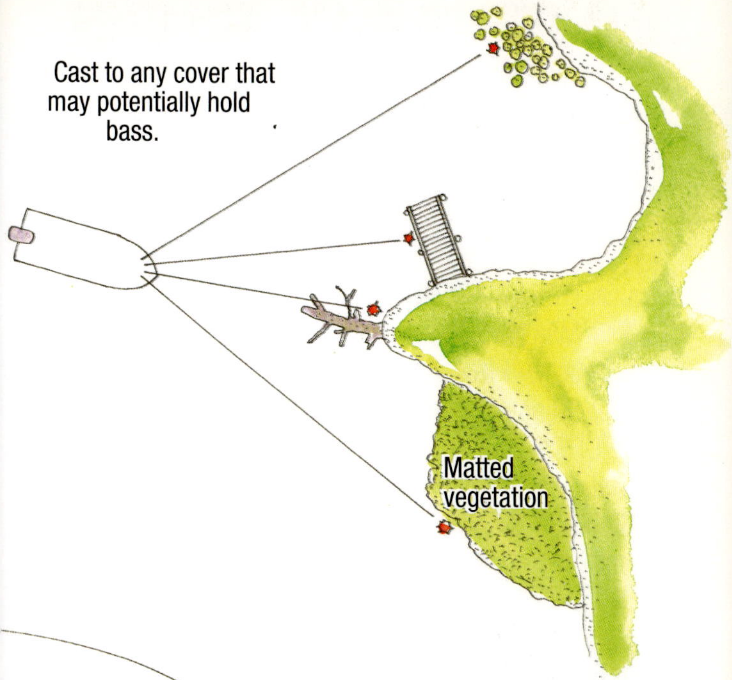

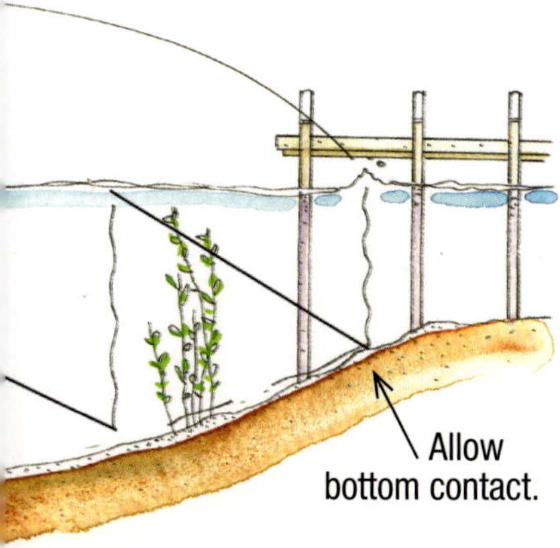

TIP

Cast a Wacky Rig around isolated cover during the spawn to entice big lazy female bass into biting.

LIVE BAIT RIGS

LIVE BAIT RIGS FOR BASS

CONTROLLED DEPTH RIG
- Bait-Minnow

CAROLINA RIG
- Bait- Minnow/Leech/Worm/Frog

DROPSHOT RIG
- Bait- Minnow/ Leech/Worm

SPINNER RIG
- Bait- Minnow/ Leech/Worm

JIG
- Bait- Minnow/Leech/Worm/Frog

SLIPPED BOBBER or FIXED BOBBER RIG
- Bait- Minnow/Leech/Worm

BOTTOM BOUNCER RIG
- Bait- Minnow/Leech/Worm/Frog

LIVE BAIT RIG (Plain hook attached to main in line with no weight)
- Bait- Minnow/Leech/ Worm/Frog

KNOCKER RIG
- Bait- Minnow/Frog